Favourite Irish Recipes

Traditional Fare from the Emerald Isle

Index

- Almond Cheesecakes 30
- Apple Pudding 35
- Baked Salmon 24
- Balnamoon Skink 13
- Barm Brack 11
- Beef in Stout 7
- Blackcap Pudding 10
- Boxty Pancakes 21
- Carageen Pudding 16
- Champ 31
- Cockle Soup 45
- Cod and Cockles 15
- Cod's Roe Fritters 39
- Colcannon 8
- Dublin Coddle 47
- Honey Pudding 22
- Hunter's Pie 37
- Irish Coffee 23
- Irish Farm Broth 6
- Irish Roast Rabbit 38
- Irish Stew 3
- Leek and Oatmeal Broth 29
- Michael Kelly's Sauce 34
- Oatcakes 5
- Parsnip and Apples 26
- Pork Ciste 40
- Potato Soup 19
- Potato Wine 42
- Potted Herrings 18
- Scallop Pie 32
- Soda Bread 27
- Spiced Beef 46
- Urney Pudding 43
- Yellow Man 14

Irish Stew

This is one of the oldest and most famous of all Irish recipes, traditionally made only with neck of lamb, potatoes and onions, flavoured with herbs. However, in County Tipperary, a beef stew with dumplings is sometimes referred to as 'Irish Stew'.

1½ lb neck of lamb, middle or best end, cut into cutlets and trimmed
2 large onions, peeled and sliced
1 lb potatoes, peeled, sliced and weighed after preparation
2 tablespoons fresh chopped parsley and 1 teaspoon fresh chopped thyme, mixed together
Salt and black pepper
½ to ¾ pint water

Set oven to 325°F or Mark 3. Layer the lamb, onions and potatoes in a casserole dish, sprinkling the herbs and seasoning between each of the layers and finishing with a neat layer of potatoes on top. Pour in the water, cover with a piece of buttered greaseproof paper and put on the casserole lid. Cook for 2 to 2½ hours. The traditional accompaniments to Irish Stew are either pickled red cabbage or carrots. Serves 4.

If desired, Irish Stew can, alternatively, be cooked slowly on top of the stove.

Oatcakes

One of the oldest Irish foods, often served, according to a 17th century visitor to Ireland, with sheep's cheese and boiled leeks. Traditionally, after being baked on a griddle or bakestone, the oatcakes would be hardened in front of the fire, leaning on a three-legged metal stand called a harnen.

8 oz medium oatmeal **1 teaspoon baking powder**
4 oz flour **2 fluid oz water**
1 teaspoon salt **1 oz butter**

Set oven to 350°F or Mark 4. Place the oatmeal into a bowl, sift in the flour, salt and baking powder and make a well in the centre. Place the water and butter in a saucepan, bring to the boil and pour into the well. Mix quickly together, adding a little more water if necessary, to form a stiffish dough that holds together. Sprinkle with a little extra oatmeal and roll out fairly thinly. Cut into about fifteen 3 inch rounds and, using a fish slice, place carefully on a lightly greased baking sheet. Bake for 20 to 25 minutes or until golden. Cool on a wire rack and store in an airtight tin. Serve with butter, cheese, honey or jam.

Irish Farm Broth

This soup is a substantial all-in-one meal. Traditionally made with mutton or lamb and each serving topped with a floury boiled potato, it can be made with beef or ham.

1 lb neck of lamb	2 carrots, peeled and sliced
1 to 2 tablespoons dried split peas, soaked overnight	2 sticks celery, trimmed and sliced
	1 small turnip, peeled and chopped
4 to 5 pints water	Salt
2 tablespoons pearl barley	1 heaped tablespoon fresh chopped parsley
1 onion, peeled and chopped	

1 small freshly boiled potato per serving

Place the meat, peas and water in a large saucepan. Bring to the boil, skim, then cover and simmer for ½ hour. Add the pearl barley, vegetables and salt, bring back to the boil and simmer for a further ½ hour. Remove the meat and when cool enough to handle remove the bones and cut the meat into pieces. Return the meat to the vegetables and broth in the saucepan, add the parsley, adjust the seasoning if necessary, bring back to the boil and simmer for 15 minutes. Serve in soup bowls, topping each serving with a boiled potato. Serve 4 to 6.

If preferred, the pearl barley can be replaced by long grain rice and fresh peas substituted for the dried ones, both to be added for the final period of cooking time.

Beef In Stout

A stew that dates from the 19th century, when it was often made with porter, a dark brown ale which, like stout, produced a fine, dark gravy.

- **1 tablespoon oil**
- **A walnut of butter**
- **2 lb stewing steak, wiped and cubed**
- **2 onions, peeled and sliced**
- **2 tablespoons flour**
- **Salt and black pepper**
- **2 carrots, peeled and sliced**
- **½ pint stout**
- **1 teaspoon soft brown sugar**
- **Fresh chopped parsley for garnish**

Heat the oil and butter in a large saucepan and cook the meat until lightly browned. Remove with a slotted spoon. Add the onions and fry until softened. Stir in the flour and seasoning, then return the meat to the saucepan with the carrots, stout and sugar. Stir well and bring to the boil, then cover and simmer gently for 2 to 2½ hours or until the meat is tender. Serve garnished with chopped parsley and accompanied by mashed potatoes and a green vegetable. Serves 4 to 6.

If desired, a half-and-half mix of Guinness and water can be used for the gravy and a few sliced mushrooms added to the stew. Alternatively, this dish can be cooked in the oven at 350°F or Mark 4 for the same length of time.

Colcannon

Traditionally served at Hallowe'en, Colcannon would often contain charms; a ring for marriage, a horseshoe for luck, a coin for riches and a thimble or button for spinster or bachelorhood. Somewhat similar to the Scottish Kailkenny or Rumbledethumps and the English Bubble and Squeak, Colcannon was orginally made with kale, but now more usually contains cabbage.

1 lb cabbage, washed and shredded
1 lb potatoes, peeled and cut into quarters
2 leeks, trimmed and chopped

¼ pint creamy milk or single cream
Salt and black pepper
Pinch of mace
4 oz butter, melted

Boil the cabbage and potatoes in separate saucepans until cooked. Meanwhile, chop the leeks, add to the milk and simmer together in a pan for 5 to 10 minutes. Drain the cabbage and potatoes very well. Mash the potatoes, stir in the leeks and milk and then add the shredded cabbage, seasoning and mace. Combine very well, turn out into a deep serving dish and heat through thoroughly in the oven, covering with kitchen foil to prevent browning, if necessary. Make a well in the centre of the mixture before serving and pour in the melted butter. Serve each portion of Colcannon with a spoonful of butter. Serves 4 to 6.

Blackcap Pudding

Originally made with an old fashioned, almost black variety of raspberry rarely found these days, this light sponge pudding is now more usually topped with a blackcurrant cap.

½ lb blackcurrants, topped and tailed
2 teaspoons lemon juice
1 oz sugar
4 oz flour
½ teaspoon baking powder

4 oz fresh white breadcrumbs
1 oz sugar
1 teaspoon grated lemon rind
2 eggs, beaten
½ pint milk

Well butter a 2 pint pudding basin. Rinse and lightly drain the blackcurrants and place in a dampened saucepan with the lemon juice and sugar. Cook very gently for 5 to 10 minutes, then spoon into the pudding basin. Sift the flour and baking powder together in a bowl, then mix in the breadcrumbs, sugar and lemon rind. Stir in the eggs, then add the milk and stir until combined well. Leave to stand in a cool place for 15 minutes, then pour over the blackcurrants. Cover with a piece of well buttered greaseproof paper and seal with kitchen foil. Place in a steamer and steam over a saucepan of boiling water for 2 to 2½ hours, topping up the water as necessary. Turn out and serve with custard or whipped cream. Serves 4 to 6.

Barm Brack

A rich, fruit-filled tea-bread, whose name means 'speckled bread'.

1½ teaspns dried yeast	Pinch of salt	1 level teaspn caraway seeds
½ pint warm milk and water mixed	1 oz butter	1 egg, beaten
Pinch of sugar	4 tablespns caster sugar	3 oz each currants, sultanas and raisins
1 lb strong white flour	¼ teaspn ground ginger	2 oz candied peel, chopped
	¼ teaspn ground nutmeg	

1 tablespoon sugar dissolved in 1 dessertspoon hot water for a glaze

Sprinkle yeast over milk/water mixture, add pinch of sugar and leave to stand in warm until frothy; about 15 minutes. Sift flour and salt into a bowl, rub in butter and stir in sugar, spice and caraway seeds. Make a well in centre and stir in beaten egg and yeast mixture, then add fruit and peel. Beat well together until dough leaves sides of bowl, turn out on to a floured surface and knead for 10 minutes until mixture is elastic. Place in clean bowl, cover and leave in warm for about 1 hour until doubled in bulk. Turn out and knead again lightly. Divide dough in half, place in two greased 7 inch round cake tins, cover and prove for about 15 minutes. Set oven to 450°F or Mark 8. Bake for 15 minutes, then reduce temperature to 400°F or Mark 6 and bake for further 20 to 30 minutes. Remove from tins and tap base of loaves; they will sound hollow if fully cooked. Glaze and return to oven for further 2 to 3 minutes. Cool on wire rack. Serve sliced with butter.

Balnamoon Skink

Skink is an old Irish and Scots term for broth. The Scottish Cullen Skink is made with haddock, but this Irish skink is a delicate soup made with Summer vegetables, enriched and lightly thickened with a liaison of cream and egg yolk.

3 sticks celery, wiped, trimmed and finely diced
6 cos-type lettuce leaves, rinsed and chopped
4 oz green peas
4 spring onions, trimmed and chopped
1 level dessertspoon fresh chopped chives
Salt and pepper
1½ to 2 pints chicken stock
3 fluid oz double cream
1 egg yolk
Fresh chopped parsley for garnish
4 sprigs parsley, 1 sprig thyme and a bayleaf, tied together

Place the vegetables, herbs, seasoning and stock in a saucepan. Bring to the boil, then cover and simmer for 30 minutes or until the vegetables are tender. Remove the *bouquet garni*. Blend the cream and egg yolk together, add to the soup and heat through thoroughly but without boiling. Adjust the seasoning if necessary and serve in soup bowls, garnished with chopped parsley. Serves 4 to 6.

If preferred, the egg yolk can be omitted and the soup appropriately thickened with a little cornflour instead.

Yellow Man

"Did you treat your Mary Anne to yellow man, at the Lammas Fair, O?" Lammas is the harvest festival celebrated in August and this yellow, brittle toffee was traditionally eaten at Lammas Fairs in County Antrim, where chunks were chipped off from a large block and sold to customers.

1 oz butter
8 oz brown sugar
1 lb golden syrup
1 dessertspoon water
1 teaspoon vinegar
1 teaspoon bicarbonate of soda

Melt the butter in a saucepan, then add the sugar, golden syrup, water and vinegar. Stir until all the ingredients are melted, then boil until the mixture reaches the 'hard crack' stage: 290°F. This can be tested by dropping a little of the mixture into cold water, leaving for a moment, then picking it up between the finger and thumb. When the finger and thumb are separated, the thread formed between them should break sharply. Stir in the bicarbonate of soda, when the mixture will foam up and then pour on to a greased, heatproof slab, turning in the edges with a palette knife. When cool enough to handle, pull with buttered hands until pale in colour. When completely hardened, break into rough pieces.

Cod and Cockles

This dish from Galway was originally made with a young codling and on occasion the cockles would be replaced by mussels.

24 cockles
8 medium potatoes, peeled and quartered
8 shallots or small onions, peeled and left whole
4 cod fillets or steaks
Salt and black pepper
4 small sprigs thyme
1 oz butter, melted
Fresh chopped parsley and lemon slices

Wash and scrub the cockles well, discarding any that are open. Place in a saucepan with just enough lightly salted water to cover and bring to the boil, shaking the pan from time to time. Cook until the cockles have opened, then remove the pan from the heat. When cool enough to handle strain the cockles, reserving the cooking liquid and remove from their shells. Meanwhile, parboil the potatoes and shallots and drain well. Set oven to 400°F or Mark 6. Place the cod fillets in a well buttered casserole, season and top each with a sprig of thyme. Surround with the potatoes and shallots, then spoon over the cockles and pour on the reserved cooking liquid. Melt the butter and pour over. Cover with a piece of buttered greaseproof paper, seal with kitchen foil and bake for 25 to 30 minutes or until the cod fillets are tender. Remove the thyme sprigs and serve garnished with parsley and lemon. Serves 4. If preferred, any other white fish can replace the cod.

Carageen Pudding

Carageen is a seaweed found around the coast of Ireland. Also known as Sea Moss or Irish Moss, it is full of minerals and has considerable gelatinous properties.

1½ oz dried carageen
Juice and grated rind of a lemon
1 dessertspoon thick honey
1 pint cold water
¼ pint double cream
1 egg white
Whipped cream and lemon slices to decorate

Place the carageen in a basin and cover with hot water. Leave to soak for 20 minutes, discard the water and drain the carageen well. Place in a saucepan with the lemon juice and rind and honey, pour in the cold water and bring to the boil, stirring to dissolve the honey completely, then simmer for 30 minutes. Strain the liquid into a basin and allow to cool completely when it should have the consistency of beaten egg. Whisk the cream until it is thick and fold in. Whisk the egg white until it stands up in soft peaks and fold into the carageen mixture. Rinse a 1½ to 2 pint mould with cold water, pour in the carageen mixture and chill until set. Turn out on to a serving dish and serve decorated with whipped cream and lemon slices. Serves 4 to 6.

Dried carageen can be obtained from many health food shops and when used it imparts a fresh flavour without any taste of the sea.

Potted Herrings

This recipe which dates from the late 1880s, takes it name from the herrings being cooked in a fireproof pot; it is not a fish paste.

8 herrings, cleaned, de-scaled and heads and tails removed
Salt, preferably sea salt
4 bayleaves
1 onion, peeled and sliced
1 teaspoon pickling spice
Vinegar and water, mixed together

Set oven to 325°F or Mark 3. Rub the herrings lightly with salt and place in an ovenproof dish. Top with the bayleaves and onion and sprinkle over the pickling spice. Pour over just enough of the vinegar and water mixture to cover the fish. Cover the dish and cook for 30 to 40 minutes. Remove from the oven and allow the herrings to cool in the liquid. Serve cold with a little of the liquid spooned over the fish and accompanied by buttered crusty bread. Serves 4.

Potato Soup

An Irish farmhouse soup containing two traditional ingredients, potatoes and bacon.

- **2 rashers streaky bacon, de-rinded and chopped**
- **1 oz butter**
- **1½ lb potatoes, peeled, chopped and weighed after preparation**
- **2 onions, peeled and chopped**
- **1½ pints chicken stock**
- **½ pint milk**
- **6 sprigs parsley, tied together**
- **Salt and white pepper**
- **¼ pint single cream**
- **1 rasher streaky bacon, de-rinded, chopped and fried until crisp and also fresh chopped parsley, for garnish**

Fry the bacon in a saucepan until the fat begins to run, then add the butter, potatoes and onions and cook, stirring, for 10 minutes. Add the stock, milk, parsley sprigs and seasoning, bring to the boil and then cover and simmer for 30 to 40 minutes, or until the vegetables are tender. Allow to cool slightly, remove the parsley sprigs, then purée the soup in a liquidizer. Return to a clean saucepan, stir in the cream and heat through thoroughly, without boiling. Serve in soup bowls, garnished with the chopped fried bacon and the chopped parsley and accompanied by soda bread or oatcakes. Serves 4 to 6.

Boxty Pancakes

"Boxty in the griddle, Boxty in the pan; if you can't make Boxty, you'll never get a man." Boxty is a potato bread, traditional to Northern Ireland, the mixture of which can also be converted into pancakes.

1 lb old potatoes, weighed after peeling	**¼ pint milk**
Salt and white pepper	**6 oz self raising flour**
½ oz butter	**1 teaspoon baking powder**
	1 small egg, beaten

Cook half the potatoes in boiling, lightly salted water until tender. Grate the remaining potatoes into a bowl. Drain the cooked potatoes well, season with salt and pepper and mash with the butter. Mix the grated potatoes with just over half the milk, then beat in the mashed potatoes. Sift the flour and baking powder together, then combine with the potato mixture to form a soft dough. Mix the egg with the remaining milk and stir into the dough to form a soft, dropping consistency, adding extra milk if necessary. Drop spoonfuls of the mixture on to a heated, well greased griddle or thick-based frying pan and cook for 3 to 4 minutes on both sides or until golden brown. Serve hot with butter.

Buttermilk was sometimes used in place of the egg and milk mixture to make these pancakes, which were often eaten sprinkled with sugar.

Honey Pudding

This unusual steamed pudding comes from Ulster.

¾ pint milk
6 oz porridge oats
2 oz caster sugar
2 tablespoons clear honey
1 oz butter
½ teaspoon ground cinnamon
3 eggs, separated
Finely grated rind of a small orange or a lemon

Pour the milk into a saucepan, bring to the boil then sprinkle over the oats and cook, stirring for 5 minutes. Add the sugar, honey, butter, rind and cinnamon and combine well. Separate the eggs. Remove the mixture from the heat and beat in the yolks. Whisk the whites until they stand up in soft peaks and fold into the mixture. Turn into a buttered 2 pint pudding basin, cover with a piece of well buttered greaseproof paper and seal with kitchen foil. Place in a steamer and steam over a saucepan of boiling water for 2 to 2¼ hours, topping up the water as necessary. Turn out on to a heated dish and serve with warm honey and cream. Serves 4 to 6.

Irish Coffee

"Cream, rich as an Irish brogue; Coffee, strong as a friendly hand; Sugar, sweet as the tongue of a rogue; Whiskey, smooth as the wit of the land."

Irish Whiskey	**Strong black coffee**
Sugar	**Double cream**

Warm a stemmed whiskey glass and pour in one third of a glass of Irish whiskey. Add 1 to 2 teaspoons sugar, then fill to about 1 inch of the rim with hot, strong black coffee. Stir to dissolve the sugar then top up with 1 tablespoon of double cream, pouring it gently into the glass down the back of the bowl of a teaspoon. Do not stir, but drink the Irish Coffee through the cream.

Baked Salmon

In Ireland the salmon is considered the King of Fish and there is an Irish blessing which says, 'May you be as healthy as the salmon'. Although poaching is the most usual Irish way of cooking salmon, Baked Salmon provides a rich dinner party dish.

A 4 to 4½ lb whole fresh salmon, cleaned, trimmed and de-scaled
1 shallot or very small onion, peeled and quartered
6 sprigs of fresh parsley
A walnut of butter
Salt and white pepper
¼ pint white wine or dry cider
½ pint double cream
Juice of half a lemon
Parsley sprigs and lemon slices for garnish

Set oven to 350°F or Mark 4. Place the onion and parsley sprigs in the salmon cavity and place the fish in a well buttered ovenproof dish. Dot with butter, season, then pour over the wine or cider. Cover and bake for 15 minutes to the pound, basting from time to time. About 15 to 20 minutes before the end of the cooking time pour over the cream. Carefully place the cooked salmon on a serving dish and keep warm. Strain the liquid into a saucepan and reduce slightly, stirring all the time. Add the lemon juice, heat through and pour a little over the salmon. Serve the remainder separately in a sauceboat. Garnish the salmon with parsley sprigs and lemon slices and serve accompanied by boiled potatoes and peas. Serves 4 to 6.

Parsnip and Apples

In the 17th century it was remarked that "the Irish feed much upon parsnips" and in this recipe parsnips are combined with apples to make an appetising accompaniment to roast pork.

1 lb parsnips, peeled and chopped
1 lb apples (cooking or dessert) peeled, cored and sliced

A good-sized walnut of butter
Pepper
Pinch each of ground cinnamon, cloves and nutmeg

Boil the parsnips in water until quite soft and cook the apples in a separate saucepan with *only just* sufficient water until they are soft also. Drain the parsnips well and combine with the apples, mashing them together until smooth. Stir in the butter, pepper and spices and heat through, if necessary, before serving with roast pork. Parsnip and Apples is a sauce which also goes well with roast duck.

Soda Bread

Although Soda Bread can be found throughout the British Isles, it is most closely associated with Ireland, where it is sometimes referred to as Soda Cake. The round loaves were traditionally baked on a griddle over a peat fire.

1 lb wholemeal flour	1 teaspoon bicarbonate of soda
8 oz white flour	1 oz rolled oats (optional)
1 teaspoon salt	Approximately ½ pint buttermilk

A little beaten egg to glaze (optional)

Set oven to 425°F or Mark 7. Combine together in a bowl the flours, salt, bicarbonate of soda and rolled oats, if desired, then stir in sufficient buttermilk to make a soft dough. Turn out on a lightly floured surface and knead *very* lightly before shaping into a round loaf. Place on a buttered baking sheet and, using a floured knife, slash the top with a cross. Glaze with beaten egg, if desired. Bake for 20 to 30 minutes or until the loaf sounds hollow when tapped on the base. Serve warm, cut into slices with butter.

White *'special occasion'* Soda Bread can be made by replacing the wholemeal flour with white, making 1½ lb of white flour in all. Soda Bread should always be prepared as quickly as possible and handled very lightly in the process. It is not a 'keeper' so, by tradition, it should be fresh baked every morning.

Leek and Oatmeal Broth

This is a very old soup recipe, traditionally served during Lent.

1 pint milk
1 pint chicken or vegetable stock
A walnut of butter
3 rounded tablespoons oatmeal
Salt and pepper
4 leeks, trimmed, washed well and cut into 1 inch rings
2 tablespoons fresh chopped parsley
A little single cream for garnish (optional)

Mix the milk and stock together and pour into a large saucepan. Add the butter, bring to the boil and then add the oatmeal, stirring well. Return to the boil, then simmer for 10 minutes, stirring from time to time. Add the leeks and seasoning, return to the boil, then simmer for a further 15 to 20 minutes, stirring in the parsley a few minutes before the end of the cooking time. Serve in soup bowls, garnished with a swirl of cream, if desired. Serves 4 to 6.

If desired, this soup can be puréed in a liquidiser before serving, but it is more usual to serve it 'chunky'.

Almond Cheesecakes

Irish cooks have always enjoyed making sweet dishes and in the 18th century almonds became a popular ingredient for puddings, creams and cheesecakes.

8 oz prepared shortcrust pastry
2 oz butter
3 oz sugar
3 eggs, beaten

4 oz blanched almonds, finely chopped
Juice and rind of half a lemon
1 dessertspoon rosewater
A little sifted icing sugar

Set oven to 350°F or Mark 4. Roll out the pastry on a lightly floured surface and use to line 15 to 20 lightly buttered tartlet tins. Cream the butter and sugar together in a bowl until light and fluffy, then add the beaten eggs a little at a time. Fold in the almonds, lemon rind and juice and rosewater and divide the mixture equally between the tartlet tins. Bake for about 20 minutes or until the filling is set. Remove from the tins and cool on a wire rack. Dust with sifted icing sugar and serve the cheesecakes accompanied by whipped cream.

Champ

A favourite with children, Champ is remembered in the rhyme, "There was an old woman who lived in a lamp; she had no room to beetle her champ"; a beetle being a pestle once used to mash potatoes. It is also known as Cally, Pandy or Poundies and, in Ulster, young nettle tops, parsley or peas were sometimes added to the mixture.

1 lb potatoes, peeled and quartered
8 spring onions, trimmed, but retaining their green tops
¼ pint creamy milk
Salt and black pepper
4 oz butter, melted

Boil the potatoes in lightly salted water and drain *very* well. Cover with a clean teacloth to absorb the steam and keep warm. Chop the spring onions finely, add to the milk and boil together in a pan for a few minutes. Mash the potatoes and season well, then pour in the milk and spring onions and beat well together. Divide the mashed potato between 4 warm bowls, make a well in the centre of each and pour in melted butter to make a pool.

Traditionally Champ is eaten with a spoon, each spoonful of mashed potato being first dipped in the butter.

Scallop Pie

This Ulster fish pie is traditionally served individually in scallop shells.

4 prepared scallops
1 lb haddock fillet, skinned and chopped coarsely
1 small onion, peeled and chopped
Freshly ground black pepper
¾ pint milk
Bouquet garni of parsley/bayleaf

1½ lb potatoes, cooked
2 oz butter
Salt and black pepper
3 oz mushrooms, wiped and sliced
1 oz flour
3 tablespoons single cream
1 tablespoon dry sherry

Separate red corals from scallops and reserve. Cut white meat into slices and place in pan with haddock, onion, herbs, pepper and ½ pint of the milk. Bring to boil, then simmer very gently for 15 minutes. Add corals and simmer for further 5 minutes. Remove herbs then drain well, reserving liquid. Mash potatoes with remaining ¼ pint milk, 1 oz of the butter and seasoning. Fry mushrooms in a pan with the remaining 1 oz butter, then stir in flour. Add reserved liquid, bring to boil, stirring, then simmer for 2 to 3 minutes, until thickened. Add cream, sherry and fish mixture and combine well, seasoning to taste. Set oven to 350°F or Mark 4. Divide mixture between washed, lightly buttered scallop shells, or turn into 2 pint pie dish. Top with mashed potato, dot with butter and cook for 20 to 25 minutes or until potato is golden brown. Serve with peas and carrots. Serves 4.

Michael Kelly's Sauce

Born in Cork around 1790, Michael Kelly was a composer who, in 1822, became Director of Music at the Theatre Royal in London's Drury Lane. This piquant sauce, named after him, is traditionally served with crubeens (pigs' trotters) or with tripe, but it also makes an excellent accompaniment for steak.

1 tablespoon brown sugar
1 teaspoon mustard powder
1 teaspoon freshly ground black pepper
2 tablespoons garlic vinegar
A good ¼ pint prepared white sauce
Pinch of ground nutmeg
1½ oz butter, melted

First make the white sauce. Melt a walnut of butter in a saucepan, blend in a dessertspoon of flour and cook for about half a minute. Remove from the heat, stir in a little milk to blend smoothly, then gradually stir in a good ¼ pint of milk. Return to the heat, stirring continuously, until the sauce has thickened. Mix together the sugar, mustard powder, black pepper and garlic vinegar and then stir them into the white sauce. Add the ground nutmeg and melted butter and warm through, but do not allow the sauce to become 'oily', though if it does, add a little iced water to 'cut' it. Season the sauce with salt, if desired, before serving.

Apple Pudding

This warming Winter recipe dates from the 19th century.

4 cooking apples, peeled, cored and sliced	4 oz shredded suet
½ lb flour	Grated rind and juice of a small lemon
¼ teaspoon baking powder	2 oz butter
Pinch of salt	4 oz sugar
	2 heaped tablespoons apricot jam

Sift the flour, baking powder and salt together into a bowl, then rub in the suet and add sufficient cold water to make a firm dough. Roll out on a lightly floured surface and use two-thirds to line a buttered 2 pint pudding basin, reserving the remaining pastry for the lid. Cook the apples together with the lemon rind and juice, butter, sugar and jam until soft, but still holding their shape. Allow to cool a little then spoon into the basin. Cover with the remaining suet pastry, wetting and sealing the edges well. Cover with buttered greaseproof paper and seal with kitchen foil. Place in a steamer and steam over a saucepan of boiling water for 1½ to 2 hours, topping up the water as necessary. Before serving, wrap a white table napkin around the basin and serve the pudding straight from this, accompanied by cream or custard. Serves 4 to 6.

Hunter's Pie

In many parts of Ireland, mashed potato was used for pies in preference to pastry.

Oil or dripping	**1 pint rich brown stock or gravy**
1 carrot, peeled and chopped	**3 lb potatoes, peelcd and quartered**
1 onion, peeled and chopped	**A walnut of butter**
1 stick celery, trimmed and chopped	**Salt and black pepper**
8 lamp chops, wiped and trimmed	**A little milk and butter (optional)**

Set oven to 350°F or Mark 4. Heat the oil or dripping in a frying pan, lightly brown the vegetables, then place in an ovenproof dish. Lightly brown the chops in the remaining fat, then place on top of the vegetables. Bring the stock to the boil and pour over. Cover and braise for about 30 minutes or until the chops are tender. Drain the chops and allow to cool. Strain the stock and reserve. Boil the potatoes in lightly salted water, mash well with the butter and use just over half to line a buttered 2 pint pie dish, pressing well to the sides and base. Place the chops in the pie dish, season well and top with the remaining potato, roughing it up with a fork. Brush with a little milk and dot with butter, if desired and bake for 20 to 30 minutes or until golden brown. Bring the reserved stock to the boil and, just before serving, make a hole in the top of the pie and pour in some of the stock, serving the remainder separately in a gravy boat. Serve with carrots and a green vegetable. Serves 4.

Irish Roast Rabbit

This rabbit is not roasted at all, but is casseroled in the oven!

1 rabbit, jointed	**2 onions, peeled and chopped**
Vinegar and water mixed	**4 rashers bacon, de-rinded and chopped**
2 tablespoons flour	**1 dessertspoon fresh chopped parsley**
½ teaspoon dry mustard	**½ teaspoon fresh chopped thyme**
Salt and black pepper	**½ pint milk**
2 oz butter	

Soak the rabbit joints in the vinegar and water for about 30 minutes. Drain and pat dry on kitchen paper. Set oven to 375°F or Mark 4. Mix the flour, mustard and seasoning together and coat the rabbit joints. Melt the butter in a frying pan and lightly brown the rabbit joints on both sides. Place in an ovenproof casserole. Fry the onion in the remainder of the butter until soft, then add to the casserole with the bacon and herbs. Heat the milk until just below boiling point and pour over. Cover and cook for 1 hour. Serve with boiled potatoes, carrots and a green vegetable and accompanied, if desired, with parsley sauce. Serves 4.

Cod's Roe Fritters

Cod's row is in season in February and March and, served with bacon, these fritters were a popular breakfast dish around the turn of the 19th century.

1 lb cod's roe, cooked, peeled and cut into slices
A little flour
1 egg, beaten
A little oil or bacon fat
Back or streaky bacon rashers

Grill or fry sufficient bacon rashers as maybe required and keep warm. Dust the slices of cod's roe with flour, then dip in the beaten egg. Heat the oil or bacon fat in a frying pan and fry the cod's roe slices on both sides until golden. Serve at once, with the previously cooked bacon rashers. Serves 4 to 6.

Cod's Roe Fritters can also be served as a light supper dish on buttered toast and garnished with lemon wedges and parsley sprigs.

Pork Ciste

Ciste is an old word meaning coffin which was the original name for a pie.

4 pork chops, wiped	3 carrots, peeled and sliced
3 pork kidneys, skinned and cored or 6 oz pork liver, wiped	1 dessertspoon fresh chopped parsley
Butter or oil	½ teaspoon fresh chopped thyme
2 onions, peeled and sliced	Salt and black pepper
	½ to ¾ pint pork stock

FOR THE CISTE

8 oz flour   Salt   Milk as required
1 teaspoon baking powder   4 oz shredded suet   2 to 3 tablespoons sultanas

Trim chops, leaving bone-ends free of fat, then chop kidneys or liver. Heat butter or oil in a pan and lightly brown chops on both sides. Remove, drain and place around inside edge of a medium saucepan, bone-ends sticking up. Lightly fry kidney or liver and vegetables, then spoon within the chops. Add herbs and seasoning and pour over enough stock to cover vegetables. Bring to boil, cover and simmer for about 30 minutes. For the Ciste: Sift together flour, baking powder and salt, then stir in suet. Add sufficient milk to make a firm dough, then mix in sultanas. Roll out into a circle that will just fit the saucepan. Press down so the bone-ends protrude, then cover with buttered greaseproof paper and the lid, leaving space for ciste to rise. Simmer for about 1 hour. Cut ciste into wedges and serve with the meat and vegetables. Serves 4.

Potato Wine

It is said that the Scots learned the art of distillation from the Irish, but as well as distilling Irish whiskey, Ireland also produced illicit 'poitin' or 'mountain tea' from a wide variety of alcohol-yielding ingredients, including potatoes. Potato is one of the most traditional home-produced country wines and can possess quite a 'kick'.

2 lb potatoes, scrubbed well
2 lb raisins, washed in
    hot water and chopped
4 lb brown sugar
1 pint fresh wheat, husks removed
6 pints water
Wine yeast
Campden tablet

Sprinkle the yeast granules into a cup of boiled tepid water, cover with clingfilm and leave to stand for about an hour. Grate the potatoes into a fermentation bin then stir in the raisins, sugar and wheat. Bring the water to the boil, pour over the ingredients and stir well until all the sugar has dissolved. Cover and leave to cool. When cool, add the activated yeast, cover loosely and keep in a cool place for 3 weeks, stirring at regular intervals. Strain the liquid into a demi-john topping up to 1 gallon with cold boiled water if required. Fit an airlock and leave to ferment. When fermentation has ceased, siphon the wine into a clean demi-john and add 1 crushed Campden tablet. Bung tight and store for at least six months. Finally, siphon into sterilised bottles, seal tightly and then, before drinking, take care to judge the potency of the brew!

Urney Pudding

This steamed pudding, flavoured with jam, comes from Northern Ireland.

4 oz butter
3 tablespoons sugar
2 eggs
A few drops vanilla essence

4 oz flour
1 teaspoon baking powder
2 heaped tablespoons red jam: raspberry, strawberry etc.

Cream the butter and sugar together in a bowl. Beat the eggs lightly and add to the mixture a little at a time, combining well between each addition. Stir in the vanilla essence. Sift the flour and baking powder together and fold into the mixture. Warm the jam slightly over a basin of hot water if at all stiff, and stir into the mixture. Turn into a well buttered 1 to 1½ pint pudding basin, cover with a piece of buttered greaseproof paper and seal with kitchen foil. Place in a steamer and steam over a saucepan of boiling water for 1½ hours, topping up the water if necessary. Serve with a matching hot jam sauce. Serves 4.

If desired, apricot jam can be used, in which case substitute butterscotch essence or a little finely grated lemon rind for the vanilla, and add a little lemon juice to the jam sauce.

Cockle Soup

Soups made with shellfish have always been popular throughout Ireland.

40 to 50 cockles	**¾ to 1 pint milk**
1 oz butter	**2 sticks celery, finely chopped**
1 small onion, peeled and finely chopped	**2 tablespoons fresh chopped parsley**
	Salt and pepper
2 heaped tablespoons flour	**¼ pint single cream**

1 stick celery, trimmed and finely chopped for garnish

Wash and scrub the cockles well, discarding any that are open. Place in a large pan with just enough lightly salted water to cover and bring to the boil, shaking the pan from time to time. Cook until the cockles have opened, then remove pan from the heat. When cool enough to handle, strain the cockles, reserving the liquid, and remove from their shells. Melt the butter in a pan and sweat the onion gently until soft, then stir in the flour and cook for 1 minute. Mix together the reserved liquid and milk and gradually add to the flour mixture, stirring until smoothly blended. Add the celery, cook for 5 minutes, then stir in the chopped parsley and season. Bring to the boil, simmer for 2 to 3 minutes then add the cockles and heat through thoroughly. Stir in the cream and heat gently, but do not boil. Garnish with chopped celery and serve with crusty brown bread or soda bread. Serves 4 to 6.

Spiced Beef

Eaten hot or cold, Spiced Beef is traditionally served on Christmas Day or St. Stephen's Day (26th December), decorated with holly and red ribbons.

4 lb rolled salted silverside
1 onion, peeled and sliced
1 small turnip, peeled and sliced
3 carrots, peeled and sliced
1 bayleaf
12 cloves
2 oz soft brown sugar
Juice of a lemon
½ teaspoon each ground cinnamon, allspice and nutmeg
1 level teaspoon mustard powder

Soak the meat in cold water overnight. Next day, rinse well and tie up with kitchen string to form a firm, neat joint. Put the onion, turnip and carrot in a large saucepan, place the meat on top, add the bayleaf then cover with cold water. Bring to the boil, skim, then cover and simmer gently for 3½ to 4 hours. Leave to cool completely in the liquid. Set oven to 350°F or Mark 4. Drain the meat *very* well, place in a roasting tin and stick with the cloves. Mix together the remaining ingredients and spread over the meat. Bake for 40 minutes, basting from time to time. Remove the string and serve hot or cold. Serves 4 to 6.

If desired, a little Guinness can be added to the water in which the meat is boiled.

Dublin Coddle

To 'coddle' means to 'cook slowly or parboil' and this dish of ham, sausages, onions and potatoes dates back to the 18th century.

1½ pints water
8 thick slices of ham, cut into chunks
8 pork sausages, cut into thick slices
2 large onions, peeled and sliced
1½ lb potatoes, peeled and sliced
Salt and black pepper
2 heaped tablespoons fresh, chopped parsley

Fresh chopped parsley for garnish

Bring the water to the boil in a saucepan, then add the ham and sausages and cook for 5 minutes. Drain well, reserving the cooking liquid. Set oven to 300°F or Mark 2. Place the ham and sausages in an ovenproof dish, add the onions and potatoes, seasoning and chopped parsley and pour over just enough cooking liquid to cover. Cover with a piece of buttered greaseproof paper, put on the lid and cook for 1 to 1½ hours or until the liquid is greatly reduced and the vegetables cooked but not mushy. Serve garnished with parsley and accompanied by soda bread. Serve 4 to 6.

METRIC CONVERSIONS

The weights, measures and oven temperatures used in the preceding recipes can be easily converted to their metric equivalents.

Weights

Avoirdupois	Metric
1 oz.	just under 30 grams
4 oz. (¼ lb.)	app. 115 grams
8 oz. (½ lb.)	app. 230 grams
1 lb.	454 grams

Liquid Measures

Imperial	Metric
1 tablespoon (liquid only)	20 millilitres
1 fl. oz.	app. 30 millilitres
1 gill (¼ pt.)	app. 145 millilitres
½ pt.	app. 285 millilitres
1 pt.	app. 570 millilitres
1 qt.	app. 1.140 litres

Oven Temperatures

	°Fahrenheit	Gas Mark	°Celsius
Slow	300	2	140
	325	3	158
Moderate	350	4	177
	375	5	190
	400	6	204
Hot	425	7	214
	450	8	232
	500	9	260

Flour as specified in these recipes refers to Plain Flour unless otherwise described.